Social Security Retirement Planning

You Should Have Started Your Financial and Retirement Goals Yesterday

Phil C. Senior

Social Security Retirement Planning

Bluesource And Friends

This book is brought to you by Bluesource And Friends, a happy book publishing company.

Our motto is **"Happiness Within Pages"**

We promise to deliver amazing value to readers with our books.

We also appreciate honest book reviews from our readers.

Connect with us on our Facebook page www.facebook.com/bluesourceandfriends and stay tuned to our latest book promotions and free giveaways.

Don't forget to claim your FREE books!

Brain Teasers:

https://tinyurl.com/karenbrainteasers

Harry Potter Trivia:
https://tinyurl.com/wizardworldtrivia

Sherlock Puzzle Book (Volume 2)

https://tinyurl.com/Sherlockpuzzlebook2

Also check out our best seller book

"67 Lateral Thinking Puzzles"

https://tinyurl.com/thinkingandriddles

Social Security Retirement Planning

Table of Contents

Introduction
Chapter 1: Importance of Social Security
  Importance of Social Security
  Benefits of Social Security
    Categories of Protection
    Benefits to the Worker
    Benefits to Your Family
  How Much to Expect in Benefits
Chapter 2: Earning Social Security Credits
  Social Security Credits and How You Earn Them
  How to Maximize Your Social Security Benefits
Chapter 3: Taking Early Benefits
  Can One Take Warly Benefits?
  Reasons for Claiming Social Security Early
Chapter 4: Insurance Calculation
  How to Calculate Your Social Security Benefits
  Is Your PIA Likely to Change After You Turn 62 Years?
  Age Adjustments for Social Security Begin with Your PIA
  The Formula for Reduction if You Draw Benefits Before Your FRA
  Calculating the Credit for Benefits Taken After the FRA
  How Does Inflation Impact Your PIA?
Chapter 5: Spouse Benefits
  Qualifications for Spousal Benefits

Social Security Retirement Planning

    How Much Will yYou Receive?

Chapter 6: Survivor's Benefits

    Who Is Eligible for the Survivor's Benefits?

    How Your Spouse Earns a Survivor's Benefits

    Some Other Instances

    What the Rates Look Like

    Blackout Period

    Applying for Survivor's Benefits

Chapter 7: Social Security Month Checks and Social Security Changes to expect

    Electronic Payment Deliveries

    Social Security Changes to Expect in 2019

Chapter 8: Social Security Taxes

    How Social Security Taxes Work

    The Math Behind Social Security Tax

    People Working More than One Job

    Who Are Exempted from Pay Social Security Tax?

    Keeping an Eye on Social Security Taxes

Chapter 9: Some Useful Resources

    So Where Should You Turn to for Help?

        AARP

        Social Security Works

        Center for Retirement Research at Boston

        Books

        Calculators

        Social Security Administration

Conclusion

Introduction

Congratulations and thank you for taking your time to download this book!

It is important for you to be informed about Social Security retirement planning, and how it will be of benefit to you and to your dependents once you pass on. You should plan for all the people you are likely to leave behind so you have more assurance of what will happen if you are no longer there. You are not only planning for death; you are as well planning for retirement. What will happen after you retire and you are no longer under a payroll? The decisions that you make today will give you a better life in the future.

This book gives you detailed information on Social Security and what you need to know. You will get to understand who is eligible to receive the survivor's benefits after the deceased has passed on, and you will get to understand how you can benefit as an individual paying their credits to Social Security. There are processes and rules that survivors need to adhere to so that they will be able to access the funds. You will be able to find this information in this book.

The information on this book is deemed to be truthful and the author of this book has researched via different sources on the internet so as to compile the available information. There are other books on the same topic; however, you have chosen to download this book and make it your source of information, and for that, thank you very much.

I hope this book will serve its purpose in giving you the knowledge you require on the this topic. Read on and be informed!

Chapter 1: Importance of Social Security

Social security is a term used to describe a government program or system that makes use of public funds in order to provide economic security to the public at a certain level. The Social Security program by the United States government was started in 1935. It was formed to provide disability, old age, and survivors insurance as well as supplementary income for the disabled and the elderly in society.

Both employers and employees in the United States are required to submit social security taxes. The money raised is then used to provide benefits to those who have attained the retirement age or are eligible based on the mandate of the program. Basically, those working today provide funds to those drawing out the benefits today, and workers today will draw benefits from workers later.

Social security benefits are based on the amount that you paid over your productive years, and how much you pay is calculated based on your income. The greater the income you have, the greater the benefits you will draw out. However, for people earning low incomes, Social Security also provides a disproportionate amount. In essence, Social Security is a program that provides for the needy in society. Every person is provided with a Social Security number. The purpose of this number is keeping track of your contributions to the program and enable you to get the benefits that you are entitled to. It is therefore important to ensure you are an active contributor to the program so as to enjoy the benefits.

Importance of Social Security

Social security is important for all Americans. Studies show that 54 million Americans depend on Social Security; that is one in every six persons. Approximately two in every three senior citizens depend on Social Security for a sizable amount of their income while a third of seniors depend on the benefits for about 90% of their income. The average benefit annually is $13,000. The benefits of Social Security may be modest but they are very important.

This is the most important method for the government to protect workers and their families against loss of income if a worker is disabled severely or retires. It also protects when a parent or a spouse dies or is made disabled. The Social Security program helps to alleviate poverty. If this program did not exist, 45% of seniors would be poor against the current 10%.

There are many benefits of Social Security that can be categorized for the retired, disabled, and survivors.

Benefits of Social Security

When most people hear about Social Security, they usually assume it is about a monthly check for when they retire. However, it is important to know that the benefits of Social Security are a lot more than just retirement benefits. As earlier discussed, there are benefits should one become disabled, and if you die, there are benefits to your dependents and benefits for medical care. These benefits are not dependent on your retirement because you are able to enjoy them if needed way before you retire. To help you understand these benefits, take a look at these facts:

- In 2014, about 3.3 million children were beneficiaries of Social Security;
    - ✓ 350,000 received because of a retired parent
    - ✓ 1,634,000 because of a disabled parent
    - ✓ 1,245,000 because of a deceased parent
- 34% of Social Security benefits are channeled to the children and spouses of deceased, disabled, or retired workers.
- The average age of a disabled worker is 54 years
- Statistics show that one in four 20-year-olds today will be disabled before attaining the age of 67.

These risks are real and Social Security comes in to help families that have faced the loss of income, either through death or an injury that may cause permanent disability. If you want to plan and protect for the future against possible risks, it is important to understand how the benefits work and how they apply. This information gives you adequate knowledge to enable you to make a decision on how you can protect your family.

Categories of Protection

There are two categories of available benefits through this program that will help you manage pre-retirement risks. These are:

- Worker benefits
- Worker's family benefits

These benefits are very important for your overall financial planning.

Benefits to the Worker

Apart from retirement benefits, there are two other benefits of Social Security to the worker, these are medical cover and income cover in the event that you become disabled.

Should you become disabled, depending on your history as a worker, you can be eligible for one or two benefit programs: Supplemental Security Income (SSI) or Social Security Disability Insurance (SSDI).

The SSDI usually pays some amount of your pre-disability income based on a certain complex formula. To qualify for SSDI, it is dependent on your medical condition and work history. In essence, you must have worked for at least ten years although there are many exceptions that are based upon one's age.

To know how much to expect from the disability payment, you need to look into your Social Security benefits statement and see what your full benefit on your retirement age is. This is going to give you an idea of what to expect; however, you must keep in mind that there are various factors that will affect the number of benefits to be received. Another benefit is that you may be eligible for Medicare health insurance after being disabled for 24 months.

Benefits to Your Family

In case of death or disability, there are certain benefits that will be available to your children and spouse.

A spouse is only eligible for benefits of Social Security under the following circumstances:

- If the spouse is caring for your children or child under the age of 16
- If he/she has attained the age of 62 years, or 60 years for survivor benefits
- If the spouse is disabled and over the age of 50 they will receive survivor benefits

Another factor for eligibility of these benefits for a spouse is if you were married for at least a year, while the requirements to benefit for survivor benefits is 9 months only. However, it is important to note that there are various exceptions to the requirements on the 9 month marriage length.

For children, they are likely to benefit in case of your disability or death. The children that stand to benefit are biological, legally adopted, or a dependent stepchild. There are circumstances that determine the eligibility of the child receiving benefits, and these are:

- The child should be unmarried
- Must be under the age of 18 years
- Can be 18 to 19 if a full-time student in high school through grade 12

- If the child is over 18 years and is disabled, with a disability that happened before the age of 22

How Much to Expect in Benefits

If we assume that every member qualifies for benefits, they will be likely to receive up to:

Spouse:

In case of death, a spouse is qualified for 100% of your Full Retirement Age benefits if:

- They are at their full retirement age
- They are caring for your child under the age of 16 regardless of the spouse's age

A spouse who is surviving is eligible to request for the benefits at the age of 60 but the benefits received will be reduced.

Should you become disabled, your spouse qualifies for 50% of your benefits at your full retirement age, at their full retirement age, or if they are caring for your child who is below 16 years of age. A spouse is also eligible to file at the age of 62 but the benefits are usually reduced.

Upon your death, your child is eligible to receive 75% of your benefits at full retirement age. If you get disabled, your child can get 50% benefits of your full retirement age. Benefits for children usually continue until the age of 18 or if they get married but there are exceptions, like when the child is completing secondary school, and then the benefits can run up to the age of 19. Benefits to children also continue if the child was disabled prior to the age of 22.

From the discussion above, it is clear that having Social Security is very important and the benefits are numerous, not only for when you retire, but even when you are at an active productive age. Your loved ones also benefit greatly from your Social Security, and in case of disability or death, your family is still provided for as they adjust.

Should you depend solely on Social Security?

Paying your Social Security checks is a way to prepare for your retirement. However, it is important for you to ask the most important question, can you fully depend on Social Security after retirement? According to research, only a third out of the 61.6 million people depend entirely on the Social Security they receive each month. The other population does not entirely depend on the checks; they have other sources of income. Social security ensures that the senior citizens are able to cater for themselves, and it empowers them in that they are able to cater for their daily needs.

There are some changes that have been occurring in the Social Security scene and they interfere with how Social Security benefits are distributed. There is a rise in population over the recent decades and hence there is a high number of people who expect to benefit from Social Security planning. There are a large number of people who are retiring and not enough people to replace them. This may come about as a result of school dropout cases amongst other reasons. Does this mean that one should not plan ahead through Social Security?

After retirement, you will need every bit of cash, and it would be great if it came from different sources. An average retired person is likely to receive a check of around thousand dollars a month. This is a huge boost when it comes to paying bills and paying for household expenses. However, a retired person would have a less worrisome life if they also had another source of income such as a side business.

Chapter 2: Earning Social Security Credits

For a person to be eligible for the Social Security retirement benefits, one must ensure they have high earnings in order to meet the minimum requirements. Unfortunately, not every kind of income will qualify as Social Security earnings. In case your income comes from unqualified sources, your benefits of Social Security will be negatively affected, because it will reduce your eventual retirement income and may affect your quality of life in your old age. It is therefore important to focus on making an income that will increase your benefits.

Social Security Credits and How You Earn Them

The Social Security administration uses your work credits as a measurement that helps them decide if you have accrued enough money to be eligible for the benefits. A person needs a minimum of 40 work credits in order to qualify for the benefits of Social Security. In 2017, a person needed to earn at least $1,300 to get a single credit and is allowed to earn up to 4 credits annually. However, not every kind of income qualifies you to earn a credit. In order to accrue your credits, you must ensure you focus on sources of earnings that give you credit. Some of these sources are:

1. **Salary not beyond the social security tax limit**

When you go through your pay stub, you are likely to notice that your employer has withheld some funds as taxes for your Social Security. However, note that not all Social Security taxes will be applied to your whole salary. In 2017, the limit for Social Security tax was $100,000 a year. If you earned more than that, then anything above the set limit does not attract the Social Security tax.

Any salary you earn in a year that is over the annual limit does not earn you more credits, so it will not increase your Social Security benefits. To earn one credit, you need to earn $1,300 and you can only earn up to 4 credits a year. This means that if you are earning $100,000 a year, you have already gained your 4 credits and it is not possible to earn more credits in a year.

2. Commissions and tips

This is good news for those in sales because commission and tips qualify as wages for the purposes of Social Security. Every commission and tip you earn will help you to get more work credits, and it is also counted in your earning records, helping increase your retirement benefit amount eventually. Cash tips of at least $20 in a month will be counted as work credits, but this is only possible if you report this kind of income while doing your federal tax returns which is also a requirement.

3. Vacation and severance pay

In case you get laid off and you had a severance package, at least you are assured that your Social Security benefits increase. Equally, if you terminate your employment with accumulated vacation pay and the HR department decides to cash out the vacation pay for you, this also qualifies as wages that will earn you Social Security credits.

The three above discussed ways are the only ones that earn you Social Security credits, but investment income, gifts, and loans do not earn you any credits.

How to Maximize your Social Security Benefits

The required minimum credits to earn your benefits is 40 work credits. This means that you do not need to earn more work credits in order to qualify for the minimum benefits. Nevertheless, it is important to maximize your acceptable sources of income so that you can maximize your benefits for Social Security.

To calculate your retirement benefits, Social Security takes the 35 years that you reported the highest earnings and finds an average. In case you have less than 35 years of recorded income or some of the years you earned very little, it is advisable to add your earnings by working longer in order to eliminate those years from your record.

For instance, if you worked for 32 years, the Social Security will take the total of the 32 years worked and add zero income for the 3 years. They will then find the average earnings for each year and that is how they will pay you. This clearly shows that your expected earnings will go down because of the years you did not work, but if you want your earnings to go higher, then you must work to compensate for the missed years so that you can maximize your annual benefits.

Based on the information here, it is important to ensure that a lot of your income comes from areas that earn you credits. This is not to say that other earnings are bad, but it is important to ensure you maximize on your benefits by earning credits, and that you maximize your income annually.

Chapter 3: Taking Early Benefits

Can One Take Early Benefits?

The Social Security program is designed so that you can enjoy your full benefits after your full retirement age at 66 years. However, it is possible to start getting your benefits earlier at 62 years of age, but the amounts received will be less than you will receive if you wait for your full retirement age.

Should you opt to start receiving your benefits early, the reduction on the benefits is usually based on the number of months that you want to receive the benefits before your full retirement age. At the age of 66, you shall receive 100% of your benefits. However, at 62 years, your benefits may reduce by 25%, at 63 years by 20%, at 64 years at 13.3%, and at 65 years at 6.7%.

Should you decide to work after you start receiving benefits, your benefits may be withheld if you report excess earnings. There are rules that apply to earnings for each year. This special rule means that Social Security cannot hold back your benefits for any whole month that you are considered retired, regardless of your earnings annually. Social security will also recalculate your benefits in order to give credit for months you do not receive benefits because of your earnings.

Knowing how much you stand to lose if you opt to receive your benefits before your full retirement age, why then would a person opt to lose than to wait for full benefits?

Reasons for Claiming Social Security Early

1. **Believing that you may not reach the retirement age**
   Your health is one of the many factors to consider when deciding the age you would want to claim your benefits. The average life expectancy for an American is 70 years. A person may feel that they will not reach that. Consider this, you have two people born the same year with similar work history and earnings, and one decides to draw their benefits at the age of 62, while the other opts to wait to start at 70 years of age. The one who starts early receives less in monthly payouts because of the deductions, but for 8 years before the other person. The one who starts at 70 years will receive more in monthly benefits but later.

   If you calculate their approximate earnings, if they both get to the age of late 70s, you will realize that their lifetime benefits or payouts will be the same regardless of when one starts receiving their payouts. Based on this analysis, if you have a health condition that could likely shorten your expectancy of life, it may be a smart move to claim your benefits early in order to maximize what you may be paid over your lifetime.

2. **You do not expect Social Security to help you make ends meet**
It may make sense to claim your Social Security benefits early, if you believe that you have saved enough for retirement and whatever amount you receive from your Social Security benefits will not make much of a difference in your livelihood. Statistics show that most American retirees will and do depend on the benefits of Social Security, but about one in every 10 Americans is able to save enough over their lifetime, which enables them to not need benefits from the Social Security program. If you are among this minority group, claiming your benefits early may make, sense because it may give you the income you need to pursue your hobbies or for taking a <u>vacation</u>. The second benefit, if you are in this category, is that you might reduce your annual federal income tax, although by a small amount.

3. **Your earning capacity is limited or you have no other source of income at all**
It is possible to find yourself with no income at all or your sources of generating an income are limited. In order to be able to pay your bills and survive, it may be a good idea to claim your benefits early.

However, fortunes may change. In case you get a job and you no longer need your Social Security benefits, you can fill another form called Form SSA521 to stop receiving the benefits. This can only be done within 12 months of receiving your monthly benefits, and you are expected to pay back all that you received from the Social Security program and go back to growing your benefits. This form can be filled by anyone who regrets claiming their benefits early, regardless of the reasons why as long as it is within the stipulated time and they are able to pay back what they received.

4. **Heavily Indebted**

   Debt among senior citizens is worrying. Research has shown homeowners aged 65 and above who are still carrying a mortgage has increased from 22% in 2001 to 30% in 2011. The case is even worse for those aged 75 years and above with the percentage increase having doubled. Student loans are also affecting senior citizens. According to a report from the government accountability office, student loan borrowers aged 65 and above has increased by 385%. The aggregate student loans owed by the senior citizens has jumped from $2 billion in 2005 up to $22 billion. It, therefore, may be advisable to draw out your Social Security benefits early in order to help pay debts.

5. **If you are the lower-earning spouse**

   It also would make sense to start getting your benefits early if you earn less than your spouse. Ideally, you and your spouse must come up with a plan that will yield the best benefits from the program in the long run. You may plan to allow the larger income of the two to grow so that the larger payout may accrue to 8% annually, meaning a bigger benefit in the long run. A couple can decide to use the benefits they seek earlier on to pay their bills, while they maximize on ensuring with the other spouse's income, they build toward their retirement benefits.

6. **You believe you can grow your money more than 8% per year**
   Holding out on receiving your benefits usually earns you an interest of 8% annually. If you are sure you have a sure way to invest the money and earn much more than the 8%, then it may make sense to withdraw your benefits early. Some people may opt to invest in stocks, but the market is not consistent. It is not common for people to request for their benefits due to this reason but in case they do, it is important to make sure that your investment will pay off.

7. **You are worried about the issues facing Social Security**
   In case you foresee trouble in the program, taking Social Security benefits early may make sense. Based on the latest reports from the board of trustees, the program is likely to start eating into its $2.9 trillion reserves of assets. This kind of news may cause anxiety to some senior citizens, so they opt to get their benefits early. However, it is important to note that Social Security will keep paying its beneficiaries regardless of the cash they have, because the benefits are out of payroll taxation, and because of the benefits of taxation, the beneficiaries will surely get their benefits.

Based on the information in this chapter, you now know that it is possible to take early benefits from your Social Security benefits. You are also aware of the consequences of this decision should you choose it, and the circumstances under which many may opt for early drawdown of their benefits.

Chapter 4: Insurance Calculation

There is a complex formula that is used to calculate your Social Security benefits. Some of the factors that go into the calculations are:

- The length of time you have worked
- How much is your annual income?
- Inflation rate
- The age at which you begin to take your benefits.

There are steps for how you calculate your benefit amount. In these steps, you will be able to notice how the above four factors affect it.

How to Calculate Your Social Security Benefits

To calculate the amount of benefits you will receive, there is a three-step process to it.

- First step: use the history of your earnings in order to calculate your AIME (Average Indexed Monthly Earnings)
- Second step: using your AIME, you can now calculate your Primary Insurance Amount, (PIA)
- Third step: Use the PIA and adjust according to the age you will start benefits

First Step: Calculating Your Average Indexed Monthly Earnings (AIME)

To calculate your benefits, you start by looking at how long you have worked and how much you earned each year. This is what is referred to as the earning history. To calculate your AIME, you take the highest earned years to a total of 35 years of your earnings history.

a) Have a list of your earnings over the years. You will only pick the earnings that are within the annual limit. The annual limit is called Contribution and Benefit Base
b) Consider inflation yearly and adjust your earnings accordingly. A process known as wage indexing is what Social Security uses to determine inflation on your earnings. There are two steps in the wage indexing process:
   1. The Social Security publishes each year the national average wages. This list is available at the National Average Wage index page
   2. Your earnings are indexed to the average earnings for when you turn 60. For each year, take the average income of your indexing year, divided by the average income for the year you want to index; from the answer, multiply it with your included earnings

   The wage indexing formula works in such a way that if you are not yet 62, your calculations to determine your benefits will not be accurate, but an estimate. Without being certain of your average wages at the time you turn 60, it may not be possible to do an accurate calculation. However, you can make an assumption of the expected inflation rate, add it to the average wages in order to estimate your average earnings in the coming years, and use this to come up with an estimate.

c) You can also calculate your monthly average by using your indexed earnings of the highest 35 years. Social security uses 35 of your best earning years to come up with your monthly benefits. In case you have less than 35 years in income, a zero for the missing years is used in the calculation, meaning that the average will be lowered. Once you get the total of the highest earnings in the 35 years, divide by the number of months found in those years, 420 months. What you get is what is referred to as Average Indexed Monthly Earnings (AIME).

Second step: Calculating Your Primary Insurance Amount (PIA) Using Your AIME

After determining your AIME, you put the resulting figure into a formula so as to determine your Primary Insurance Amount (PIA). This formula is based on bend points. The formula for Social Security benefits is designed in such a manner that it gives a higher proportion of income to low-income earners than higher income earners. In order to achieve this, the formula uses what is termed as 'bend points.' They are also adjusted in accordance with inflation each year.

Bend points starting from when you turn 62 are used to calculate your retirement benefits. For instance, if you are using AIME of $4569, this is how you calculate:

- The first $826 of AIME, take 90% of it
- Next $4,980 AIME take 32%
- Lastly, 15% of the amount exceeding $4,980

Total the answers you get and that is your PIA, the amount you will benefit from if you begin getting benefits at the Full Retirement Age (FRA). Usually, the PIA is rounded to the next lower dime and the benefit amount is also rounded to the next lowest dollar.

If you haven't reached the age of 62, the calculations of your benefits are usually approximations, because you may not yet know the bend point amounts for when you turn 62. However, it is possible to come up with your approximate PIA by using approximate bend points too.

Is Your PIA Likely to Change After You Turn 62 Years Old?

The answer is yes. There are two factors that may cause this change. These are:

1. Higher earnings – if your earnings between the age of 62 and 70 increase and are higher than those of the 35 years used to calculate previously, then your AIME will change; it is this that is used to calculate your PIA, hence your benefits will change if your earnings increase
2. Inflation – the cost of living adjustments applied to individuals already receiving their benefits will also apply to your PIA in the same manner. Because of this factor of inflation, it is safe to conclude that your PIA is also likely to change

Third Step: Adjusting Your PIA for When You Will Begin Benefits

The last amount of benefits that you receive is based on when you begin benefits.

- We have already established that the earliest age at which you can begin to receive your retirement benefits is 62 years, and at age 60 if you are qualified for a widower or widow's benefits
- You will also stand to get higher benefits if you wait longer before you begin

With this, another complex formula is also used.

Age Adjustments for Social Security Begin with our PIA

The Primary Insurance Amount (PIA) is the amount you get when you start benefits at your Full Retirement Age (FRA). The formula for adjustments begins by taking into consideration your PIA. FRA varies according to the year one was born. For those that were born between 1943 and 1954, their FRA age is 66. It is important to note the following;

- There is a percentage reduction that is applied to your PIA if you begin drawing benefits before your full retirement age
- There is a credit called delayed retirement credit if you opt to begin receiving your benefits after your FRA

The Formula for Reduction if You Draw Benefits Before Your FRA

- 5/9 of 1% per month is how your benefits are reduced for up to 36 months, all dependent on the number of months you have before your FRA
- 5/12 of 1% of your benefits are reduced if you have more than 36 months before you reach your FRA. If the number of months is more than 36, the formula also changed further. This then means that if your FRA is 66 years and you begin drawing benefits at 62, then your PIA is reduced by about 25%

Calculating the Credit for Benefits Taken After the FRA

This is calculated very simply. It is usually 2/3 of 1% a month or 8% annually. This means that should you exceed your FRA of 66 and decide to draw your benefits later, your benefits are going to increase by 2/3 of 1% or by 8% annually. Survivor benefits for spouses also benefit from the delayed benefits. This is calculated monthly or annually for every delayed benefit. This, therefore, translates to mean that if your FRA is 66 but you decide to wait until 70 to benefit, your benefits will have increased by 32%.

How Does Inflation Impact Your PIA?

Your PIA is usually calculated at the age of 62. If you opt to wait beyond this age, for each year beyond 62, adjustments due to the additional cost of living will apply to your PIA. This is usually based on a 2% inflation rate. If you are near 62 years, the benefit amount at the age of 70 will be much higher due to the adjustments caused by the cost of living or inflation. Many people fail to put this into consideration when they do their calculations and opt to benefit early, when it is best to wait until your FRA or even after.

Calculating your benefits is very complex. Before you make a decision on whether to start benefits early or wait longer, it is important to be sure you have done the correct calculation so as not to be misled. It is advisable to seek services of a professional to help you understand and even calculate your benefits, and hence, be in a position to make a more informed decision.

Chapter 5: Spouse Benefits

In the event of death, their Social Security benefits are available to their current or former spouse. The Social Security benefit to a spouse is called 'spousal benefit.' This benefit is available to:

- A current spouse
- A widowed spouse or
- An ex-spouse

Qualifications for Spousal Benefits

Current spouses are eligible for spousal benefits as well as an ex-spouse, if they were married for at least 10 years and did not remarry after the divorce prior to getting to 10 years. You must be at the age of 62 to receive a spousal benefit.

If both spouses are alive, you are not eligible to apply for spousal benefits until your partner first files for them.

However, the rules are different for ex-spouses. An ex-spouse is able to receive spousal benefits based on the records of the ex-partner, even if the ex-partner has not applied to receive their benefits yet. However, your ex-partner must at least be 62 years old or more. It is important to note that taking a spousal benefit does not in any way affect the number of benefits your spouse, ex-spouse, or ex-spouse's current spouse will receive when the time comes.

How Much Will You Receive?

A spouse can claim Social Security benefits based on their own earnings or can receive 50% of the amount of their spouse's benefits at FRA. The Social Security uses the higher amount to calculate. You can benefit based on your own records of earnings or based on your spouses' records of earnings. A spouse can decide to apply for benefits based on their own earnings at 62 or FRA and delay the other benefits based on their spouse's earnings at the age of 70. This is a smart way to spread your benefits and maximize on them. This means that at the age of 70, you can switch from earning benefits from the lower earnings and get the higher earnings.

This is one of the biggest advantages of Social Security. When most people reach the age of 60, they slow down and are not as active or productive. At the age of 62, many of them are ready to take it slow, and the benefits come in handy. The double benefits to spouses are also good, because it ensures that they are still able to cater to their needs and live a quality life even after retirement.

Chapter 6: Survivor's Benefits

The Social Security benefits can be offered to those left behind. In order for the person to reap the benefits of Social Security funds, they must have worked long enough under Social Security. The survivors include the widow, widower left behind, children, and grandchildren.

Who Is Eligible for Survivor's Benefits?

The widow or the widower left behind

The widow and the widower who has been left behind by the beneficiary is eligible to receive the benefits. In order for the spouse who has been left behind to qualify, they have to be at the age of 60 years or more. Under special circumstances such as disability, even if the spouse is at the age of 50 they will still receive these benefits. If the widow is left behind with the children of the deceased and they are taking care of them, then they will be eligible and age will not be considered as a factor.

Parents of the deceased

If the parents were dependent on the deceased, they are eligible to receive survivor's benefits. This will occur if the parent is 62 years and above. The percentage changes depending on the existence of both parents. If only one of the parent was dependent on the child they will get 82.5 % of the benefit, and, if the both of them are dependent then they will get 75% of the survivor's benefits.

An ex-husband or wife

If the spouse who was once married to the deceased had a marriage which lasted 10 years or more, they are eligible as well. The rules regarding age will also apply in this case.

Children of the deceased

If the deceased has a child who is under the age of 18 years old and they are not married,, they are entitled to receive the benefits. If the child is at the age of 22 years but is disabled they are also entitled to the benefits. In special circumstances, the stepchildren, adopted children, and grandchildren can get survivor's benefits.

How Your Spouse Earns a Survivor's Benefits

Throughout the working lifetime of the individual, they will not need more than 40 credits. The 40 credits add up to ten working years of the individual. The amount of money the survivors earns will depend on the number of years that the individual has been working as well as their age. If an individual dies at a young age, then the survivor's benefit will be low compared to when an individual passes away at an older age.

When a person dies, the Social Security office should be notified immediately. However, most of the times the Social Security office will be notified by the funeral home. It is good to note that you cannot apply for survivor's benefits online, and that you have to visit their offices in person and discuss the benefits that you are eligible to receive.

There is a once off death benefit that can be paid to the surviving spouse, and if the spouse is not present, then it will be given to one of the deceased children depending on eligibility.

There are some instances that will cause changes in the survivor's benefits. If your spouse was receiving monthly benefits and they pass away, you are supposed to return the amount of money that was paid for the month of death or any later month. How you pay back the money will depend on the method in which the deceased received the funds.

If the funds were being received via direct deposit in the bank or other financial institution, you should contact them and have them give back the amount that has been credited to the deceased's account. If the amount was being received via check, do not cash the check, but return it to the Social Security office.

You should not use any of the funds that are for the deceased in the month of death or the final months as well.

Some Other Instances

If you were receiving benefits as the spouse of the deceased before they passed away, your benefits will be converted into survivor's benefits once your spouse dies.

If you remarry at the age of 60, the benefits that you are bound to receive will not be affected. The same case applies if you remarry at the age of 50 years and you are disabled.

If you have a child with the deceased who is disabled and under 16 years of age, even if you get married at an earlier age, it will not interfere with the benefits that you receive. It also will not be considered if your marriage lasted a ten-year period or not. However, the child in question has to be the biological child of the deceased or they have to be legally adopted.

The one-time death benefit of $255 has its own special circumstances under which it can be received. The amount can be received by the spouse if, by the time of death, they were still living in the same household. The spouse can still receive the sum if they were living apart at the time of death. However, some factors will have to be considered. One of the factors is if they were already receiving benefits and it was evident on the worker's record. The other factor is if the spouse has become eligible after the death of the deceased. If there is no eligible living spouse, the amount can then be paid to the child of the deceased or their children. The requirements for receiving the one-time amount are the same as those of the spouse.

What the Rates Look Like

The actual amount you receive depends on the amount of money the deceased made over their lifetime, subject to the Social Security payroll taxes. While determining the exact amount one is entitled to can be tough, so here are some guidelines to help you estimate the amount you are entitled to.

If neither you nor the deceased had started benefits yet and you wait until their full retirement age before applying for the benefits, you will get 100% of their basic benefit. If the deceased was past retirement age and had not commenced taking their Social Security benefits yet, you may be entitled to higher benefits corresponding to that later age.

If you file for the benefits between the age of 60 and the deceased full retirement age, you will get between 71 and 99% of their basic benefit amount. If you haven't reached the full retirement age and decide to go ahead to collect the survivor's benefits, you may lose some of your benefits by continuing to work as you may surpass the limits.

If you and your deceased spouse were already receiving benefits, you will receive the larger of the two amounts and not both. And if you are caring for a child under 16 years of age, you will receive 75% of the deceased benefit amount.

Blackout Period

This is the period in which beneficiaries are unable to collect their benefits. They come as a result of inconsistencies in the rules that govern the benefits that parents, offspring, and spouses are entitled to. The inconsistencies often arise due to the differences in the ages that have to be attained before someone claims the benefits. For instance, a beneficiary spouse can only collect the benefits they are entitled to at 60.

But they can collect the benefits the children of the deceased are entitled to.

Life insurance is the most common remedy for the blackout period. The insurance provides coverage for a certain amount of predetermined time, usually between 15 and 30 years. Basically, life insurance gets a survivor death benefits up until the time they are eligible to collect their Social Security benefits.

Applying for Survivor's Benefits

As you can tell from the eligibility requirements, the Survivor's Benefits claim cases vary widely. This makes it almost impossible for applications to be done online. As such, applications for the benefits are normally done over the phone or by physically visiting the local Social Security office in your area.

The requirements to file an application include:

- Proof of death through a funeral home or providing a death certificate
- The Social Security number of the deceased and the beneficiaries
- The birth certificate of the beneficiary
- Your marriage certificate if you were married to the deceased
- The Social Security number of dependent children
- The federal self-employment tax return W-2 forms for the recent year

- The bank name and number where the money will be deposited to

You will be required to provide specific documents depending on your situation and how you were related to the deceased.

It is important to provide accurate and valid information during your application for a smooth and seamless procedure. Normally, your local Social Security office will try to verify your information with the Bureau of Vital Statistics in your area. The accuracy of your information makes the process smoother and less cumbersome.

Chapter 7: Social Security Month Checks and Social Security Changes to Expect

Normally, Social Security Retirement benefits are paid one month after you have been deemed eligible to receive the benefits. For instance, if your first month for Social Security benefits is January, you can expect the deposits to be made in your account in February.

Deposits are usually done on either the second, the third, or the fourth Wednesday of the month. The actual day is dependent on your day of birth. This is how the payments are scheduled:

- If you are born between 1st and 10th, your payments will be made on the second Wednesday of the month
- For those whose birthdays fall between the 11th and 20th, your payments will be processed on the third Wednesday of the month
- For those whose birthdays are between the 21st and 31st, their security checks are processed and deposited on the 4th Wednesday of every month

Sometimes the dates may not be the same. For instance, if you are to receive your Social Security benefits and your SSI payments together, you can expect your Social Security check to come a little bit early; normally the third day of the month. Another important exception to note is during holidays. If your Social Security check is scheduled for a holiday, then you can expect your check to be deposited a day earlier.

Electronic Payment Deliveries

As from the first of March 2013, the Social Security moved from paper checks. Presently, monthly checks are sent directly to beneficiaries' bank accounts or through the debit card option. These are more efficient, more convenient, safer, and more reliable options as compared to the previous mode of check delivery.

For the people who still receive their Social Security checks via mail, there are some instances where the checks may delay for a few days. This is one of the setbacks that come with having the checks delivered via mail. In the event of a delay, just wait for a few days and check with the mail guys if they have your check coming. If the check does not arrive after several days, you can call Social Security and report your missing check. Alternatively, you can find a Social Security office near you and go there for some assistance.

The best way to avoid such delays is by having your Social Security benefits deposited directly to your bank account.

Social Security Changes to Expect in 2019

Every year in the month of October, SAA (Social Security Administration) makes its annual changes in the program. As per the announcements made in 2018, these are the changes that will affect Social Security through 2019.

1. 2.8% payment increase

The 2.8% increase in the payment affects all the 67 million Social Security beneficiaries. The reason for the increase is to counter the inflation effects. This is a 0.8% increase from the amount that was payable last year. However, this increase amounts to $39 per month for an average recipient and an increased payout to $1,461 from the previous $1,422 in 2018.

2. The wage base will increase to $132,900

The wage base has also been raised from the $128,400 in 2018 to $132,900 in 2019. Any earnings above that amount will not be taxed. The tax rate, however, still remains at 6%.

The increase in the wage base also means that the maximum amount used to determine the retirement benefits also increase. The Social Security benefits for a person at full retirement age will increase by $73 from the previous $2,788 to the current $2,,861.

3. The continued increase in the age of full retirement

Keeping up with the "increasing" trend, the full retirement age, also, goes a little higher. The earliest one can start claiming their benefits is after attaining 62 years of age. Earlier claims result in a permanent payout reduction. Full retirement now stands at 66 years and 4 months. In fact, it is stated that the full retirement age is set to increase every year by at least two months until it hits 67. This means that if you were born past 1960, your full retirement age now stands at 67 years.

4. Increased earnings limits

If you commence collecting your Social Security benefits while still working, part or all of your Social Security benefits may be withheld depending on the amount of money you earn. The income limits, however, are set to increase this year 2019. Prior to reaching the age of full retirement, you can earn up to $17,640. From there, you will be deducted $1 for every $2 in excess of the limit. At full retirement, you will earn $46,920, up from $45,360 in 2018. Every $3 earned above your limit attracts a $1 reduction. This, however, only applies to money earned months before you hit your full retirement age.

5. Increased Social Security disability threshold

The Social Security disability threshold are also increasing in 2019, although slightly. For legally blind persons, they will receive $2040 every month. This is a $70 increase from the amount they received in 2018. As for the non-blind persons, their maximum benefit will increase by $40, from the previous $1,980 to $1,220 in 2019.

6. Online COLA Notices

An improvement made in the Social Security scene effective 2019 is that people registered under the program are now able to view their COLA notice through an online platform. All you have to do is simply log on to your mySocialSecurity account and you are good to go.

This is a significant improvement from the past where notices were sent via mail. While the mail notices haven't been scrapped completely, people have a choice to receive their notices via mail or online.

Chapter 8: Social Security Taxes

A Social Security tax is a type of tax that is levied on both employees and employers. The tax is used to fund the Social Security program. Social security tax is collected in for self-employment tax or payroll tax. It pays for disability, retirement, and survivorship benefits that millions of Americans receive every year.

How Social Security Taxes Work

Basically, the Social Security tax is applied to the income of employees and self-employed people. For those who are employed, employers usually withhold a certain amount, as per the set percentage by the government, from the paychecks of their employees and forward that amount to the government. The amount is not usually put in trust for specific employees paying into the system. Instead, the amount collected is used to pay the current retirees and those who are entitled to survivorship benefits.

In 2018, the Social Security tax rate stood at 12.4%. This rate was applicable to all wages for the employed and income for the self-employed. For employed persons, employers were required to collect half of the total amount due (6.2% of the wages) on behalf of the government from their employees' pay. The other half was to be paid to the government by the employees themselves.

As for persons who are self-employed, they were required to pay both the full 12.4% of their income to the government to go into the Social Security program. 12.4% is calculated from their net earnings and not their business profits. For the self-employed, the self-employment tax includes Medicare and Social Security taxes.

The good thing about being self-employed and paying the self-employment tax, is that you can claim an above-the-line deduction for half of your tax on the Form 1040's first page as an income adjustment. This means you can get back the employer half of your Social Security tax offering you some tax relief.

The Math behind Social Security Tax

How it works is that there is a wage base that has been set. So all self-employment income and wages that are up to the wage base set for a given year are subject to the Social Security tax. The wage base has been progressively increasing over the years. Since 2012, the wage base has increased from $110,100 to $128,400 in 2018. There was a steep increase between 2016 and 2017 where the wage base increased from $118,500 to $127,200.

Well, this is how the math works,:

If you earn anything less than $132,900 which is the set wage base, you multiply your earnings by 6.2 percent to know the amount that you and your employer each must pay to the Social Security program as part of the tax. If you are self-employed, you have to pay the whole amount by yourself. To know the amount you have to pay, multiply your net income by the set rate of 12.4%.

If your income is above $132,900, multiply this wage base by the current rate of 12.4% to know the amount payable to the Social Security program. Again, the employed will pay 6% of their wages, while their employers deduct the remaining 6% of their wages and send it to the government. For the self-employed, they will calculate 12.4% of the $132,900. Any amount earned above the wage base is tax-free.

People Working More than One Job

If you happen to have more than one job, you are not obligated to pay the Social Security tax above the wage base. As such, you should keep your wage base in mind. For instance, if your wages for all your jobs exceed the set wage base, then it is up to you to inform your separate employers when you have collectively attained the set limit. Have them stop withholding your pay for a while to avoid paying extra.

Who Is Exempted from Paying Social Security Tax?

Not every person is required to pay the Social Security Tax. There are certain groups of people that are exempted from paying the Social Security tax. These groups include:

- People who belong to a religious group that is opposed to receiving he offered Social Security benefits when they retire, if they are disabled or after death.
- Non-resident aliens or person who are not citizens of the United States nor legal residents of the US, who stay in the country temporarily as students.
- Non-residents aliens who are in the US and working for a foreign government.
- Students who are employed by the same school they study where the employment is dependent on them being enrolled at the institution

Keeping an Eye on Social Security Taxes

The Social Security tax topic is a hot one. It is a very sensitive topic for policymakers and the government in general. The economy has changed significantly over the last few years, prompting policy makers to consider raising the tax to get more funds to support the program. However, there is great opposition for that move as an increase in the Social Security tax rate would hurt low-income earners.

A proposed alternative is to maintain the current rate as it is but have the benefits associated with paying the Social Security tax reduced. Again, this is unattractive to a good number of people who would love to have Social Security benefits untouched if not increased.

Well, from these issues, it is quite clear that action has to be taken sooner or later is at all a Social Security crisis is to be averted. As such, you should keep an eye on the subject. Sooner or later, some drastic changes are going to affect the Social Security tax.

Chapter 9: Some Useful Resources

Without a doubt, Social Security benefits are very instrumental in facilitating a comfortable financial life for older people and people living with disabilities. But even with that, it can be quite challenging for people to get accurate information to help then navigate the subject easily. A significant portion of the information available on the internet is incorrect or contradictory.

Most people would prefer getting in touch with the Social Security Administration for information and clarification. But even they, according to experts, often provide misleading information. Half of the responses they give to inquiries made are usually misleading or entirely wrong. In fact, the Office of the Inspector General for Social Security agency presented a report indicating that they lose about $131 million due to bad advice and misinformation.

So Where Should You Turn for help?

Well, here are the places you can get some important information from regarding Social Security retirement benefits.

AARP

The first place you can get all your questions answered correctly and satisfactorily is at AARP's Social Security

Resource Center. This resource center was launched with the aim of assisting retirees and seniors find all the information they might require with regards to their Social Security benefits.

When you visit the website's dashboard, you will be able to access links to various commonly asked questions and the main topics people always want to know about. Some of these top subjects include information regarding eligibility, work and taxes, disability benefits, benefits in general, survivor's benefits, spouses and children, divorce, and generally how to navigate SSA.

There are, also, other blogs and resources that will help you have a better understanding of the subject.

Social Security Works

Social Security Works is an advocacy organization. The organization runs a platform that contains the most frequently asked questions and their answers. The questions vary and the answers are usually very comprehensive.

Information on Social Security varies from one state to another. Social Security Works, also, provides you with comprehensive reports on the Social Security benefits as per each state. It, also, will provide you with various Social Security facts sheets to keep you informed and equipped with any information that may affect you.

Center for Retirement Research at Boston

Another resource you can use to get important information with regards to your Social Security benefits is the Center for Retirement Research in Boston. The research center produces Social Security claiming guides that cover pretty much the whole Social Security subject. The guide also comes with a section that answers the frequently asked questions in a clear format that is colorful and easy to read.

The guides come at a cost. A copy goes for $2.75 each if you are buying less than 100 copies and $2.50 if you are purchasing a hundred copies or more. The cost is inclusive of shipping costs.

Books

There are several books that extensively cover Social Security benefits available on the market. These are also very important and reliable sources of trustworthy information with regards to your Social Security benefits.

Here are some of the books you should have in your library if you want to fully understand Social Security:

- **Social Security Made Simple**
  Security Made Simple was written by Mike Piper. The book is not that long but it touches on a large number of topics with regards to Social Security. The 27 pages contain tonnes of information ranging from the eligibility requirements to how you can collect your benefits. It also addresses the subject of when one should file for their benefits. This is definitely a book everyone needs.
- **Social Security Basics: 9 Essentials that Everyone Should Know**
  This book was written by Devin Carroll and it is the best book you can get that covers all the Social Security benefits fundamentals in a detailed way. Having this book will help you master the basics. The

9 essentials have been covered in a simple yet detailed manner making it informative and at the same time, easy to digest.

- **Get What's Yours – The Secret to Maxing Out Your Social Security**
  This book was written by J. Kotlikoff, Paul Solman, and Philip Moeller. This is a must-have given it was written by experts in Social Security. And just to prove how good the book is, it made it to the New York Times list of Bestsellers. Once you have handled the first two books mentioned above and have understood the basics, this is the next book to get. The book is quite dense and more detailed further broadening your knowledge of Social Security Benefits.

- **Social Security for Dummies**
  This book was written by Jonathan Peterson. Just as the book title hints, the book dissects some of the most complex topics on Social Security and explains them in a simple language for anyone to understand. It also provides you with insights into the changes you can expect in the near future in Social Security.

- **Social Security: The Inside Story 2018 Silver Anniversary Edition**
  This book written by Andy Landis winds up the list of some of the tops books you can get yourself to understand Social Security better. Just like the other, the book is quite comprehensive yet very simple to read and understand. Given the author is a person who worked for Social Security, you can expect to get the most accurate information with regards to Social Security in this book.

Calculators

There are online calculators that can help you know when to file your claim and, also, help you figure out the amount of money you should expect as benefits.

Social Security Administration

While all the listed sources of information are valid and reliable, The Social Security Administration remains to be the best place for you to get information from given they are the ones in charge of Social Security. They have offices in every State where you can access all the information you need by simply booking an appointment. Additionally, SAA has various online calculators and produces various detailed fact sheets to help people understand Social Security benefits better.

Conclusion

If you are seeing this, then it means that you have read the book up to the end. Congratulations on finishing this very informative book. I hope the book was enlightening and that it has given value to you. It is important for you as a reader to understand more about Social Security planning and to start paying your dues earlier on so you can reap the benefits.

The book clearly talks about Social Security planning, who is eligible for it, and how much money you as the retiree is entitled to. It has pointed out the amount of money each survivor is to receive in case of death. We are glad that you have taken the time to gather your information from this book. The book was made especially for you, the reader, so you have all of the knowledge that you require concerning this topic and you can decide what to do with it.

In this book, you will see how much your survivors will receive in instances of early death depending on the number of years that you have been working. Some situations are unavoidable, and it is always better to ensure that your loved ones are catered for. We hope that this book will be a great resource to you and others you may want to share it with, and thus, will arm you with enough information on the topic.

There is a lot of information out there on this topic and if you feel that you need further guidance on the topic, it would be best for you to gather more information. Go out and seek expert opinion on this and get as many facts as possible. You can decide to visit the Social Security offices and ask questions or visit their website. Go and plan ahead for the future of your family!

Thank you for taking the time to read this book and for making it up to the end; you are appreciated for that.

If you feel that this book has added value to your life in any way and it has given you better insight on the topic, please leave positive feedback! Thank you!

Connect with us on our Facebook page www.facebook.com/bluesourceandfriends and stay tuned to our latest book promotions and free giveaways.

www.ingramcontent.com/pod-product-compliance
Lightning Source LLC
Chambersburg PA
CBHW030733180526
45157CB00008BA/3150